Electricity
FROM BENJAMIN FRANKLIN TO NIKOLA TESLA

Jenny Mason

Checkerboard
Library

An Imprint of Abdo Publishing
abdopublishing.com

ABDOPUBLISHING.COM

Published by Abdo Publishing, a division of ABDO, PO Box 398166, Minneapolis, Minnesota 55439. Copyright © 2019 by Abdo Consulting Group, Inc. International copyrights reserved in all countries. No part of this book may be reproduced in any form without written permission from the publisher. Checkerboard Library™ is a trademark and logo of Abdo Publishing.

Printed in the United States of America, North Mankato, Minnesota
052018
092018

 **THIS BOOK CONTAINS RECYCLED MATERIALS**

Design and production: Mighty Media, Inc.
Editor: Rebecca Felix
Cover Photographs: Shutterstock (center), Wikimedia Commons (left, right)
Interior Photographs: Royal Institution of Great Britain/Photo Researchers, pp. 17, 29 (top); Shutterstock, pp. 4–5, 11, 15, 19, 27; Thinkstock, pp. 13, 28 (bottom); Wellcome Images/Wikimedia Commons, p. 9; Wikimedia Commons, pp. 7, 14, 21, 23, 25, 28 (top), 29 (bottom)

Library of Congress Control Number: 2017961642

Publisher's Cataloging-in-Publication Data
Name: Mason, Jenny, author.
Title: Electricity: From Benjamin Franklin to Nikola Tesla / by Jenny Mason.
Other titles: From Benjamin Franklin to Nikola Tesla
Description: Minneapolis, Minnesota : Abdo Publishing, 2019. | Series: STEM stories | Includes online resources and index.
Identifiers: ISBN 9781532115462 (lib.bdg.) | ISBN 9781532156182 (ebook)
Subjects: LCSH: Electricity--History--Juvenile literature. | Inventors--Biography--Juvenile literature. | Electrical engineering--History--Juvenile literature.
Classification: DDC 621.3092--dc23

Contents

Electric Energy

What are the first few things you do each morning? Do you turn off a digital alarm clock and then turn on bathroom lights? Maybe you check the weather on a smartphone or get juice from the fridge. These things all **involve** electricity!

Electricity makes it possible for people to **efficiently** light, heat, or cool their homes. Refrigerators use electricity to keep foods fresh. Lights, fans, ovens, and more use electric power. And computers, cell phones, and other devices run on electricity.

Electricity is a type of energy. People first discovered electricity could be harnessed to do work in

The invention of the light bulb led to the development of the world's electrical infrastructure.

the mid-1800s. Since then, scientists and inventors completely changed how people live. Electricity is all around us today thanks to the energy grid.

The energy grid is a large, **complex** electrical system. It is considered one of the world's most impressive feats of engineering. Its power lines web the nation.

Electricity lit our way out of the past. And today's **innovators** are creating electronic **technologies** and devices that will shape our future!

CHAPTER 1

The First Sparks

The first discoveries relating to electricity date back to 600 BCE. Around this time, ancient Greek philosopher and astronomer Thales recorded a strange finding. He rubbed fossilized tree resin, called amber, with cloth. After doing so, the surface of the amber attracted certain lightweight materials. These included feathers, hair, and straw.

Thales **hypothesized** the amber was a kind of magnet. But he was incorrect. Thales had actually witnessed static electricity. This is the same charge created when you rub a balloon on your hair to make the strands stand on end. But it would take centuries for scientists to recognize and name static electricity.

In the 1600s, English physician William Gilbert did more experiments with amber. He too rubbed amber and found the **friction** seemed to magnetize the material. But Gilbert also noticed that rubbed amber sometimes gave off a spark.

Magnets did not give off sparks. So, Gilbert determined amber contained a different **invisible** force. He called this force

Gilbert demonstrates electricity experiments for Great Britain's Queen Elizabeth I.

electricus. This is a Latin word meaning "of amber." Scientists experimented with electricity into the next century.

CHAPTER 2

Capturing Electricity

Advanced understanding of electricity continued into the 1700s. In the 1720s and 1730s, English scientist Stephen Gray discovered certain materials blocked electric currents. Later scientists named these materials *insulators*. Other materials allowed electric currents to flow through them. These materials were later named *conductors*.

In 1745, Dutch scientist Pieter van Musschenbroek made an important **innovation** in Leiden, Netherlands. He used an electrostatic machine to transfer electricity into a jar of water. Van Musschenbroek later touched a metal wire placed in the water. Because metal is a conductor, the electric current flowed through it and shocked his hand! Electricity had been stored in the jar. It was the world's first device to acquire and store electric energy.

News of the discovery in Leiden spread through the global scientific community. The device was called a Leyden jar, after an alternative Dutch spelling of the city name. Other scientists created their own **versions** of Leyden jars to use in experiments.

Later Leyden jars were covered in a thin layer of metal foil. This was more effective at storing an electrical charge.

Many scientists hoped the Leyden jar would reveal how and from where electricity was created. American colonist and inventor Benjamin Franklin was one. He believed lightning was electricity. His idea was **controversial** at the time. This was because most people believed God or the gods created lightning.

CHAPTER 3

The Perfect Storm

To prove his theory that lightning was electricity, Franklin came up with the idea for an experiment.
He wanted to capture lightning in a Leyden jar during a storm. Historians disagree about whether Franklin himself performed his experiment.   But they do know he shared his idea in letters to friends. Soon, other scientists learned of Franklin's idea. In 1752, French scientist Thomas-Francois Dalibard completed it.

Dalibard braced a 40-foot (12 m) metal rod in a glass bottle outside. When a storm arrived, the rod attracted a lightning bolt. The metal conducted the lightning's energy into the bottle, which acted as an insulator and held the energy. When an assistant touched the bottle, the energy escaped as a spark! This spark proved lightning and electricity were the same form of energy.

As word spread about Franklin's proven theory, people realized electricity was a force of nature that could be stored. Franklin became known as an electricity pioneer. And other scientists began searching for ways stored electricity could be put to use.

Benjamin Franklin

BORN: January 17, 1706, Boston, Massachusetts

DIED: April 17, 1790, Philadelphia, Pennsylvania

FACT: By the time Franklin was born, he already had 14 older siblings!

FACT: Franklin was a writer, inventor, scientist, and diplomat.

ACHIEVEMENTS

▶ Franklin took part in politics. He helped write and draft the Declaration of Independence and the US Constitution.

▶ Franklin **negotiated** the 1783 Treaty of Paris. It ended the **Revolutionary War** between England and the newly formed United States.

▶ Franklin invented many things. These inventions include the first US lending library.

▶ Franklin developed the theory that lightning was a form of electricity.

▶ Franklin invented the words "battery," and "charge."

STEM Star

CHAPTER 4

Batteries

Franklin's ideas had helped scientists prove lightning was a form of electricity. Scientists were aware of other examples of electricity in nature. They had witnessed electricity in certain animals, such as the torpedo fish. These fish produce shocks to defend themselves from predators and to stun prey.

Italian physicist Alessandro Volta studied the electric organs in the torpedo fish. He found they were in a stacked pattern of discs and tissues. In 1800, Volta set out to imitate this organ in an experiment to better understand electricity.

Volta stacked two kinds of metal discs and cardboard or cloth soaked in **brine**. Brine contains **electrolytes**. When electrolytes connect two metals, a chemical reaction occurs. During this reaction, electrons move between the substances. This created a current of steady electricity in Volta's stack. And the bigger the stack, the more energy it produced. Volta created the world's first battery!

FUN FACT

The volt was named after Alessandro Volta.

Volta shared his findings with other researchers. The Voltaic pile amazed scientists. Leyden jars also held electric energy. But the level of power inside them was never **predictable**. Volta's battery gave scientists a way to produce electricity at levels they could control.

In the early 1800s, English chemist Humphry Davy used a battery to invent the arc light. It was a constant arc of light stretched between two charcoal sticks or rods. This was an important discovery. But it would take the development of a source of electric power to make electric light a common resource.

When Volta first demonstrated his battery, he called it an "artificial electric organ."

Batteries:

PAST AND PRESENT

Scientists made many improvements to the battery following Volta's invention. In the 1880s, dry cell batteries were invented. Dry cell batteries used a paste instead of liquid **electrolyte**, allowing them to be transported. Dry cell batteries are used today to power all kinds of devices! There are several types. Alkaline and lithium are among the most common and popular.

VOLTAIC PILE

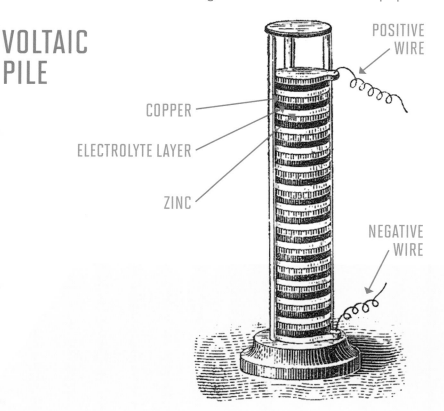

POSITIVE WIRE

COPPER

ELECTROLYTE LAYER

ZINC

NEGATIVE WIRE

DRY CELL
BATTERY

METAL CAP

ZINC CASE
(NEGATIVE ELECTRODE)

ELECTROLYTE PASTE

CARBON ROD
(POSITIVE ELECTRODE)

CHAPTER 5

The First Electric Motor

Scientists continued studying electricity using wires and metals, as Volta had. Davy's assistant, Michael Faraday, was one such scientist. Faraday also studied magnetism.

By the 1820s, it was common knowledge that magnets created **invisible** fields. In 1821, Faraday performed experiments to better understand how electricity and magnetism interacted.

Faraday made a circuit using a battery, wire, metal, stick magnet, and liquid mercury. Mercury is a metal that is liquid at room temperature. It is also a good conductor. Faraday filled a glass container with mercury and placed the magnet in it. He ran a wire from the battery to the mercury. The other wire ran from the battery to the metal stick. The stick had a metal arm or rod attached to it. Another wire hung from the arm into the mercury.

Electricity flowed from the battery through the wires, mercury, and metal stick. The invisible field around the hanging wire interacted with the magnet's invisible field. This caused the metal stick to move in circles.

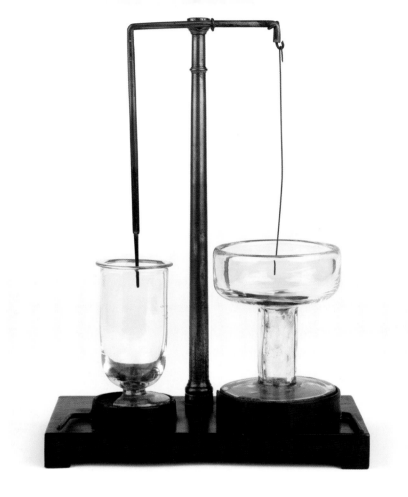

Faraday's motor is on display in the Faraday Museum at the Royal Institution in London, England.

Faraday had used electricity and magnetism to produce movement. He had created the first electric motor! This was a groundbreaking discovery. People realized electric energy could do more than make light. It could power machines!

CHAPTER 6

Electric Communication

Faraday's invention had illustrated the idea of a motor. Throughout the 1800s, scientists researched other ways electricity could be put to work. Electric **telegraph** machines were one invention. In the 1830s, US inventor Samuel Morse worked on a **version** of these devices.

On Morse's machines, the sender tapped a message on a telegraph. The message was sent over wire to a matching device. The receiving device's electromagnetic lever moved up and down to relay the message. This usually created a tapping sound. The person receiving the message wrote down the sounds in Morse code. This was a language Morse created. Combinations of short or long taps represented letters.

As Morse introduced his system to others, telegraph stations were set up around the nation. Telegraphs in these stations were connected by electrical wires that stretched for miles between cities. The machines sent messages to one another. Station workers wrote down the taps in Morse code and converted them

Today, all commercial telegraph lines and stations are closed. But some private owners still use telegraphs to communicate with one another.

into words. **Telegraphs** allowed people to communicate in minutes rather than weeks or months by mailing letters!

In the 1850s and 1860s, telegraph wires were webbed across the United States and much of Europe. By 1866, a giant telegraph wire stretched across the Atlantic Ocean. It linked North America and Europe with a bridge of electric communication.

CHAPTER 7

Let There Be Light

Morse's invention was revolutionary. In the 1870s, Scottish scientist Alexander Graham Bell made an invention that allowed **telegraph** lines to carry the sound of a person's voice. Bell invented the telephone! It forever changed the way people communicated. Meanwhile, other scientists had been working on a different **innovation** that would impact modern life.

In the early 1800s, British inventor Warren De la Rue designed an **incandescent** light bulb. It was a glass tube with a **platinum** filament, or thread, coiled between two wire posts. When an electric current passed through the bulb, the filament glowed.

Before this, people burned gas, wood, and oil to create flames for light. Light bulbs made creating light easier! Unfortunately, platinum was expensive. Most people could not afford De la Rue's bulb. So, other inventors made cheaper bulbs using different materials. But these bulbs overheated and burned out quickly.

US inventor Thomas Edison wanted to make a cheap, long-lasting bulb. He and a team of researchers tested new filaments. These included silk, cork, and even beard hair!

In 1879, Edison filed a patent for a bulb with a carbon filament. It shone for between 13 and 15 hours. This was longer than any other bulb invented. But Edison kept testing. In 1880, he found bamboo filaments glowed for 1,200 hours!

In 1881, Edison announced his idea to **implement** light bulbs for everyday use. At the time, gas lines ran to many structures. Edison wanted to replace these lines with electric lines connected to **generators**.

Edison had 1,093 patents in his lifetime!

CHAPTER 8

Power Plays

In 1882, Edison built his first electric power station. It was in Manhattan, New York. The station held **generators** connected to a gridded network of underground electric cables. The cables ran to homes and buildings outfitted with light bulb fixtures. These structures had electric light at the flick of a switch!

Edison's generators moved an electric current continually in one direction. He called this movement *direct current* (DC). DC worked well to provide power to a few nearby homes and buildings.

But DC was too slow and weak to provide power beyond one mile (1.6 km). Serbian-American electrical engineer Nikola Tesla worked on improving the system. Throughout the late 1880s, he developed a way to distribute an alternating current (AC) that was more powerful.

Tesla's AC system solved the problem of transmitting electricity to large cities and rural areas. He installed his first AC power station in 1896 in Buffalo, New York. AC quickly became the global standard. It shaped the world's power **infrastructure**.

Nikola Tesla

BORN: July 10, 1856, Austro-Hungarian Empire (now Croatia)

DIED: January 7, 1943, New York, New York

FACT: Tesla briefly worked for Thomas Edison, before establishing his own power company.

FACT: Tesla was born during a lightning storm!

FACT: The Tesla Motors car company adopted Nikola Tesla's name to honor his creativity and contribution to **technology**. The company makes an electric car that runs on a modernized Tesla AC motor.

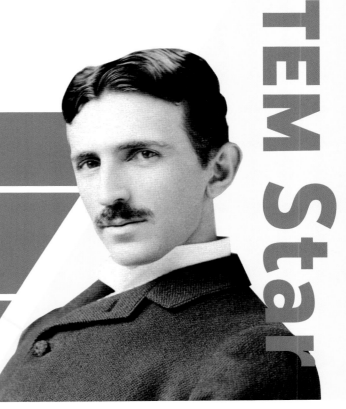

ACHIEVEMENTS

▶ Tesla harnessed alternating electrical current (AC). This enabled the world's modern power **infrastructure** to arise.

▶ Tesla created many **innovations** that influenced future electronics. His creations led to the developments of radar, laser beams, robots, remote control devices, computers, and more.

▶ Tesla designed the world's first hydropower plant. It used energy captured from the movement of a waterfall to power **generators**.

STEM Star

CHAPTER 9

Electric Expansion

With AC power transmission in place, many cities enjoyed the convenience of electricity. In 1904, another **innovation** further advanced worldwide electricity use. American inventor Harvey Hubbell II created the two-prong plug and outlet.

Plugs and outlets enabled inventors to make electric-powered devices to tackle everyday tasks and improve life. These devices included washing machines, ovens, refrigerators, and more!

Using electricity boomed in cities worldwide. In 1935, the US Rural Electric Administration formed. It loaned money to rural towns to cover the costs of installing power stations and power lines. Four years later, a quarter of rural US homes had electricity.

Scientists spent the coming years **refining** electronic devices and systems. The first television broadcast occurred in 1939. The first electronic computer was unveiled in the 1940s. And electric devices invented in the 1970s, 1980s, and 1990s grew smaller and more advanced. These devices include laptop computers, tablets, cell phones, and smartphones.

Rural Electrification Administration workers install electric lines in rural areas of the US.

CHAPTER 10

Charging Forward

Today, electricity is a part of everyday life. Amazing advancements have allowed people to use it for many tasks. In addition to providing buildings and devices with power, some modern vehicles run on electric power. Electricity is also used to power medical devices, operate machinery, and more!

While these uses of electricity are helpful, they use a lot of resources. Power plants and electric **generators** feeding the national grid often burn coal, oil, or natural gas to run. When burned, these fuels create pollution. They are also nonrenewable resources. This means they can and will run out.

Modern electricity **innovators** are working to develop cleaner, renewable sources of electric power. This includes wind turbines and solar panels. However, replacing the old fuel-burning systems with these types of energy is a slow and expensive process.

Researchers are also working to create smaller and more **efficient** electronic devices and systems. Scientists see promise in replacing the national grid with millions of microgrids. These small systems would imitate Edison's first power stations, which powered small clusters of nearby buildings. In the future, every person may become an electrical **innovator** by simply outfitting their home with the latest electronics!

Renewable energy provides 15 percent of US electricity. These energies include solar power, wind power, hydropower, biofuels, and geothermal power.

600 BCE Thales observes that rubbing amber creates an invisible force that pulls lightweight objects toward it.

1600s CE William Gilbert further experiments with amber and names an invisible force *electricus*.

1720s–1730s Stephen Gray discovers the difference between conductors and insulators.

1752 Thomas-Francois Dalibard proves Benjamin Franklin's theory that lightening is electricity.

1800 Alessandro Volta creates the world's first battery.

1821	Michael Faraday creates the first electric motor.
1880s	Thomas Edison improves the incandescent light bulb and opens the first power station to electrify homes and buildings.
1880s	Nikola Tesla introduces an alternating current (AC) transmission system.
1900s	Electronic devices such as televisions, computers, and cell phones transform daily life.
2000s	Innovators seek resources for cleaner, renewable electricity.

Glossary

brine—very salty water.

complex—having many parts, details, ideas, or functions.

controversial—of or relating to a discussion marked by strongly different views.

efficient—wasting little time or energy.

electrolyte—a liquid through which electricity can pass.

friction—the force that resists motion between bodies in contact.

generator—a machine that changes mechanical energy into electrical energy.

hypothesize—to form an idea or theory based on known facts.

implement—to put a plan or idea into action.

incandescent—glowing with light as a result of being heated.

infrastructure—the basic framework of public society. It includes a community's government, transportation, power, and education systems.

innovator—a person who comes up with a new idea, method, or device. Their creation is called an innovation.

invisible—something that cannot be seen.

involve—to require certain parts or actions.

negotiate (nih-GOH-shee-ayt)—to work out an agreement about the terms of something.

platinum—a very valuable silvery-white metal.

predictable—able to be guessed about in advance using observation, experience, or reasoning.

refine—to improve or perfect something.

Revolutionary War—a war for independence from 1775 to 1783 between Great Britain and its North American colonies. The colonists won and created the United States of America.

technology (tehk-NAH-luh-jee)—machinery and equipment developed for practical purposes using scientific principles and engineering.

telegraph—a device that uses electricity to send coded messages over wires.

version—a different form or type of an original.

Online Resources

Booklinks
NONFICTION NETWORK
FREE! ONLINE NONFICTION RESOURCES

To learn more about electricity, visit **abdobooklinks.com**. These links are routinely monitored and updated to provide the most current information available.

Index